AF323642

THEY
REWROTE
THEMSELVES
LEGENDARY

Stephens, Ronnie K.
Lee, Desarae.
ISBN: 978-0-9890092-4-9

Edited by Dane Kuttler.
Cover Art by Desarae Lee.
Layout Design by Allison Truj.

Printed in Tennessee, USA

Timber Mouse Publishing
Austin, TX
www.timbermouse.com

To contact the author, please email
ronniekstephens@gmail.com.

CONTENTS

PREFACE

This book is the culmination of a friendship that began by chance. Desarae was traveling through Ireland, sharpening her photography skills; I was in Galway for a summer writing program. On the last night of her stay in Galway, a mutual friend arranged for us to meet at The Blue Note. That particular night featured a brass band and dancing, but I couldn't tell you a single song they played. I remember exactly two things about that night: there was an elderly man who danced to every song, and friendships can form in an instant. Desarae and I were, for lack of a better word, kindred spirits. It was as though we'd been friends for several lifetimes, and we were just picking up where we'd left off.

So what does any of this have to do with the book in your hands? What you hold is a conversation. See, Desarae and I don't talk often, and we've seen each other only a handful of times since that summer night in Galway. But her illustrations spoke to me daily. And I spoke back, in the only way I knew how: through poetry. I tried to tell the stories I heard and felt when I looked at her artwork. Each time I sent Desarae one of the poems her illustrations had inspired, she commented on how precisely I had captured the history behind the image. And yes, a few times I tried to cheat; I begged Desarae for the title of a piece or the inspiration behind a particular illustration. Only once in all these years has she explained the origin of a single piece. The rest of the time, she simply remarks that she doesn't care for titles, or that she doesn't know the story behind a particular image: she just creates what she sees inside herself.

It bears noting that both Desarae and I draw on art as a form of catharsis. Both of us have struggled with anxiety and mood disorders. For us, art is a place of healing or, at the very least, a place of respite. I found the same solace in Desarae's illustrations and, I hope, she found something similar in my words. Because of that, I frequently turned to Desarae's art in my darkest moments. When I couldn't articulate my own grief, I found my voice in these pieces. And so we became friends who spoke in ekphrastics, who somehow mastered a form of collective meditation that spanned thousands of miles, who spent years in different cities without ever growing apart.

It's important for me to include that the ekphrastic form begins with art. The poetry comes after. Without Desarae's illustrations, I would not have written a single poem in this collection. Not one. I know she's too humble to admit it, but Desarae is the reason this book exists. In many instances, she is the reason I persevered. Through bipolar disorder and divorce, body dysmorphia and shifting definitions of fatherhood, I have accessed my consciousness because Desarae is simultaneously the best friend and the most talented artist I have ever encountered. I sincerely hope that my words do her illustrations justice, and that you come away with a bit of solace for yourself.

Ever grateful,

r

WHERE
THERE IS
NO AIR

FOR THE BRANCHES IN MY LOVER'S WOMB

Twenty-nine weeks I have carried this cage like a spine. I have made a home of it. My back is bent as a woman twice my age and my soles are cured leather. Dust kicks up. I pull the patchwork apron over my face and mouth. The road-weary threads have long since given way to the wind. The arthritis ticks in my joints and I know the sky is a full belly throwing shadow puppets on the ground. Your mother says the rains are here. Come and find me, sweet ones. We'll plant an orchard in the clouds. This is my gift to you. An atmosphere of bartlett pears.

DRYADS

It was always in your nature to appear
collectively, two round bodies on the ultrasound
machine at five weeks old. Your mother feared
the vanishing twin, refused to name you both
until we saw your hearts beat, watched you
bend around each other like a forest.

We had so many reasons to be scared:

the hole in your heart;
the hole in your other heart;
the tear in your lung;
the weeks you would not stay inside;

But you have strong hands, wide feet
and long bodies. Daughters born twelve years
after the doctors said I would never be a father.

You are ash tree.
You are Meliae.
You are myth.

The Greeks gave you an infant prince
and you gave back the father of the gods.

What gods will you raise this time?
What weald will you become?

BALANCE

I.

Felicity is a circus act,
a facade put on
and forced into
a little black dress
everyone notices
because it's so different
from the tool they are
used to using. Form
and function -
a false dichotomy,
to be sure.

A necessary indoctrination
for the preteens tuned in
to the CW: Smart girls
aren't strong. Smart girls
will be mocked when
they train or speak
for themselves.

Pretty girls who box
are foolish. Lost girls
who learn to fight
will die.

If you want to survive, stay inside.

Let the men handle danger
with their arrows and guns
and grunting. Be ready to love them
when they come back from battle.

II.

When they come back
from battle, remind them:

you are the one standing
on the wire; you are the one
catching them as they orbit
grief and white knight
complex like small boys
on the playground;

you are the one
at the center,
the massive,
the thing that pulls
when they run
from home.

MISCHIEVOUS MERMAIDS

I wish this were a better story.
I wish my daughters were not already stranded
in some tower. I wish there was no need
for another cautionary tale.

The first time the doctor said both babies
would be girls, I heard:

Teach them strength;
the world will assume they have none.

Teach them courage;
there is always too much dark
and not enough starlight.

Teach them loud; men will call them sirens
when their ships are splintered.

Teach them worth.
Teach them fight.
Teach them flight.

Teach them to breathe under water;
to become their surroundings.

Teach them to lock tenderness in a chest
and let it sink into a shiver of nurse sharks.

Teach them white knights will come
dressed in iron hoods and weighted suits
to claim their bodies without consent.

Swim with the current until you find
their artificial lungs. Cut them.

Let them stand like scarecrows
at the edge of the reef.

Let them serve warning:
You are not conquered.
You are conqueror.

What I said the first time the doctor spoke
    your names:

I will not let this world take from you
without permission. I will not let your story
be fantasy and uninvited boys.

But even that promise is a father
and pride and savior. I am not your savior.
You do not need to be saved.
I will sometimes forget this,
will dive into the waterlogged belly
of a clipper ship I do not captain.
Forgive me.

I wish this were a better story.
I wish it was not your lot to grow fins,
to breathe where there is no air.

I wish the first words you'd heard
were these: your body is your body.

THE ELEPHANT
IN THE ROOM

We hung in gaudy gold frames like ducks
with our fat dark lips curled and courting,
hand-me-down belles stuck in the fog
outside a school dance.

Sixteen and sure glamour
is a gallery on grandmother's wall.

But Susie knew the grace of mud stains,
harmony in skinned knees, running full tilt
and elbow wild.

She saw life for what it was - a kodiak bear
on the thinnest piece of string. A bound thing
with no memory of what it meant to break free.

DAY WATCH

blackbirds pass over head
and the leaves shout murder

murder

everywhere a blackbird
murder

her hands are fists full of rust
and the leaves shout murder

murder

NIGHT WATCH

fireflies pepper the sky
like confetti

quinn stands beneath the oak
she planted in primary school

to remind her little sister
the one born already dying

that even the smallest acorn
carries a giant in its heart

some giants stay stranded in
the clouds like banished monuments

others sneak down and steal children
making coffins of their beds

so Quinn waits with her sentry
at the top of the hill

daring the sky to let loose the monsters
coming for her sister's bones

the owl lifts itself from her palm
a fit of feathers and laughter

barking at a shiver in the tree line
down the hill

a swarm of lightning
and everything is still

Tether its flight when it is foolish enough
to grow wings. Warn of Prometheus
and the slinking moon and all of those
who fell. Who let go.

Turn your back on the sun. Sit with your knees
folded beneath you in your best dress.
Don the mask you wore to the winter
dance and still smells of your first kiss.

Square your shoulder and coax that silly thing
down. Untie the knot around your finger.
Know that it will stray too far. It will get lost
and it will get hurt. But it will not break.

It will not break.

ON THE ROAD

she stripped herself down
to shoulders and collarbone
hair pinned to the clothesline

like an ornament of sound
like a sun dress blooming
like a torso of chrysanthemums
like commodity
like do not be human
like become your art
like this is all you are

keep playing
until the bow is a bone
until the strings breathe
until its neck is your neck
until its body is your body

keep playing
when the show is over
when the train is cold and hollow
when you don't remember what city
when you don't sell a damn thing
when you can't make rent
when the birds come to rest

keep playing
keep playing

SERENADING THE BUFFALO

This room is an impossible song.

At the center: a chair,
a cello. Caroline

      bends her body round its body
      twists her spine to staircase
      ignores the sharp knot of her shoulder
      drags the bow back and forth

like a gents saw.

The wall behind her is an archipelago
of endings. Everywhere
a framed thing

      stiff-necked men
      in starched black collars
      monocles and pompadour

the beast itself.

THE ENVY OF MANKIND ON HER BACK

The sky is the last bit of this world
without a flag.

Every man dreams of claiming it.

Two brothers build and build
in the barn, play god and creation
until a bird large enough
to carry their wonder is born.

Now families crowd into hollows
made of metal and shoot themselves
into the clouds like circus acts.

Wings ripple in the wind, feathers
whitecapping in the moonlight.
She holds her feet so close
to the water it flirts with her soles.

There is something holy
about the wanting of a thing
you cannot touch, an ocean
swallowing up the stars

like a black hole
like the cannibal rage of collapse
at the middle of it all.

UNBOUND

She unlocks the gate and opens her ribs like migration. Crows burst from her chest and into the cacophony of the county fair down the hill. Everything is rising. The shrill chatter of rigged games, headlong hands on the makeshift coaster, hot air balloons full of couples losing themselves to the fog. No one can see the moon hanging over the Ferris wheel, bright as a porch light in late October. No one but Molly, breastplate wide and emptying itself like a carnival act: discontent with the caravan queue, pop-up tents and bodies still running from home.

I HAVE THIS HILL

THE BLUE NOTE

The last evening in Galway
is big bands and choreography.

I buoy against a brick wall
counting light bulbs, tracing spades
and diamonds in the wallpaper
that runs the opposite side
of the dance hall.

Across the room
a black dress dips
down past shoulders.

I have written this night
a dozen times since.

Pined over the thick blonde hair.
Fawned for the easy conversation
and the fog of our goodbye.

Sometimes there is no metaphor.
Sometimes a girl is just a girl.
My chest a chest.

Sometimes.

RAINY DAY AMONGST THE RUINS

We stayed too long. Didn't notice
the tide washing over the land bridge.

Huddled under arches and shared
umbrellas through the afternoon.
Lost time in the crepuscular purples
and greys of simmer dim.

When the stars blinked on,
we realized our mistake.

The short walk through sheep
and over sand had become
an angry sea.

We spread out along the side
of the island, searched the cliffs
for a gap small enough to leap across.

One by one, we jumped, soft hands
opening themselves against the rocks

like a prayer.

THE COUPLE STOPS AT A DINER FOR A SLICE OF PIE

I stand stiff as a sparrow,
cane hard as a tree branch
in my hand.
Your spine
bends back like a bow
hungry for hunting season.

The gears turned over
like cooked apples.

Everything is spectacle.
Everything is lost innocence.

There is a woman
tied at the ankles
hanging upside down.

You put the looking glass
to your eye.

There is a teddy bear
searching for her hands.

We watch
the last fifteen years
catch up to you like a penny
at the well of your forgetting.

There is a girl
on a witness stand.

The prosecutor pulls your name
from the case files. Sets it aside.

There is a teddy bear
searching for your hands.

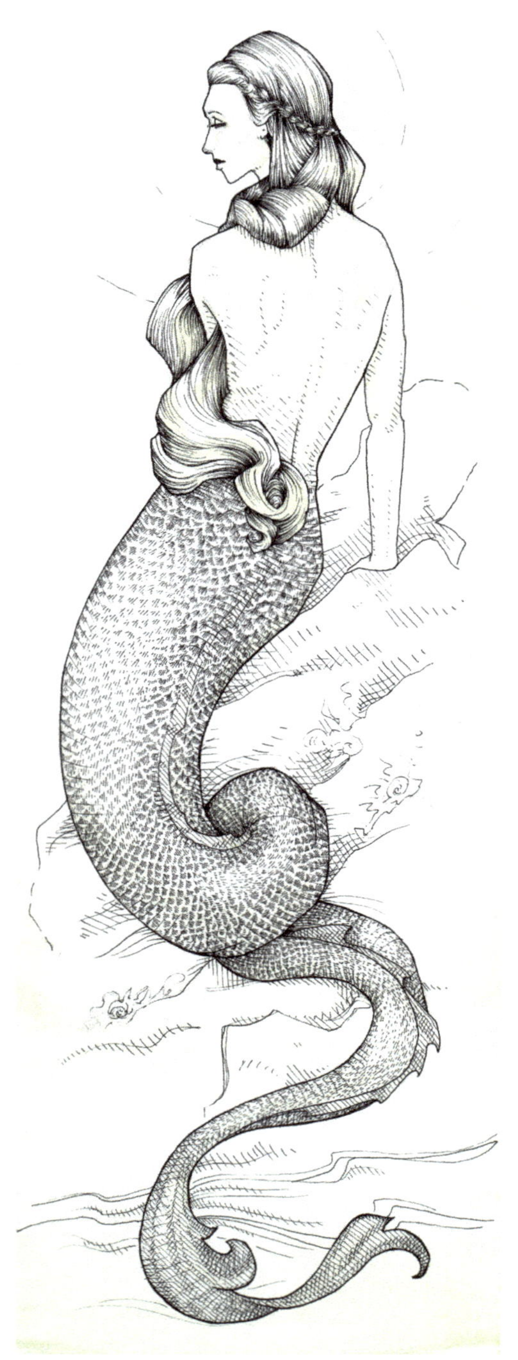

SEVEN YEARS WE PERFECTED OUR LEAVING

That first summer lingers like a moon
thin and rich as sixteenth-century halos.
Grace on commission.

We are hungry. Combing the apartment
for the RF switch, my old comforter,
the dumbbells under the bed, anything
we cannot eat, but can plead a return credit
for. There is no shame loud as empty cabinets.

The winter that follows is a warm loft,
granite counters and hardwood floors.
Blue diamond in white gold. Big wedding.
Honeymoon.

By the next summer, we are hungry again.
And so the seasons tumble over. Apartment
to house, state to state. We buy and sell
everything we ever own.

ROBOT TRIPTYCH

She made peace with the melancholy eyes,
the tambourine heart, the banjo arms stiff
and stringless at his sides.

He loved mechanically, even through the winter
she disappeared into the evergreens
behind her grandfather's house.

Didn't know what to make of the blackbirds
or the pearls around her neck. It wasn't always so.

When a marriage ends, there's rarely anything left
to say. Bodies acclimate to separate beds and weeks
without the electric pulse of someone else's skin.

She remembers first the way they held hands
in an auditorium. He remembers bluegrass and grocery stores
and cheeks sore from smiling. But that was planets ago.

Before adulthood meant function over form.
Before he shed heart and nerve and skin
to make room for productivity.

When a marriage ends, you don't really notice.
Not at first. First it is quiet as the bed and breakfast
you book after the botched proposal, every room
one word away from forever.

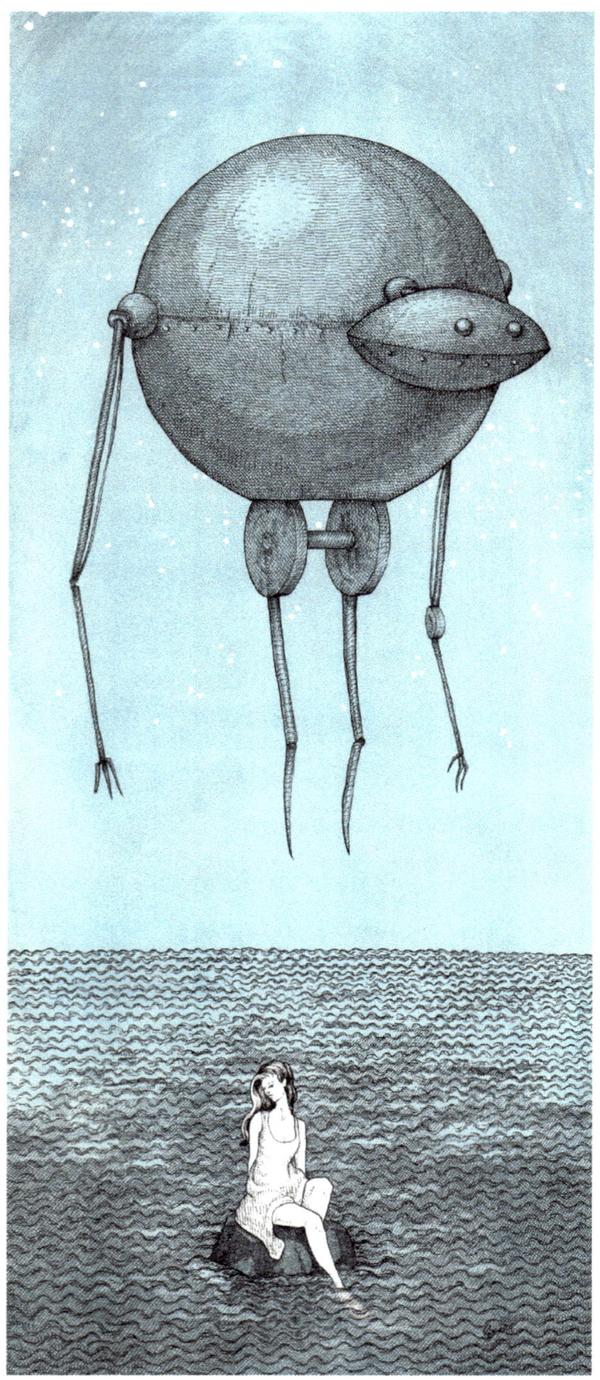

I hang in the sky like a silver ball and remember
football season, how we sat in booths over pizza
and beer, her knitting needles clicking like a hipster
bass track behind a swarm of sports fans.

Christmas is too many weeks ahead of its time.
I thought I had another month to process
our first holiday apart.

It's the week after Halloween
and at the store today,

I saw new Dove chocolate flavors
and thought of her;

I saw the R2D2 ornament
and thought of her;

I saw a purple plaid stocking
and thought of her.

She is an island, white linen and sandals,
skin like an ocean. Which is the problem,
I guess. I rust without solid ground
to stand on, and I couldn't pin myself
to this paper mache sky
without falling.

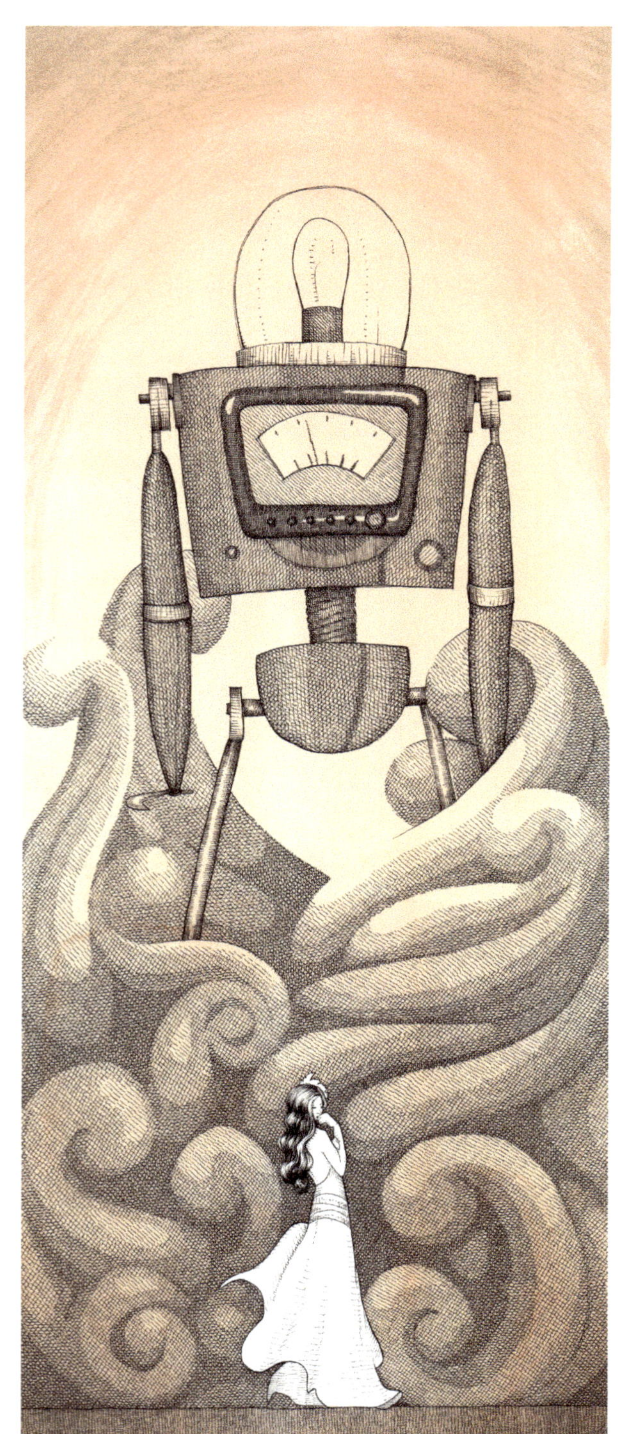

When I was seventeen a coworker
slipped GHB into my drink. Christie
was milkshake skin and bras too big
to not be noticed by men twice her age.
She was combat boots and steel-frame
Ford trucks, too, but most never knew
that side of her. Not even the boyfriend
who threatened me with a knife after
she drove me home that night.

I still don't know who did it.
But the next day doctors hooked me up
to an EKG and found that I had
an irregular heartbeat. A rhythm prone
to starting and stopping. All this to say
I have known for quite some time
that my love is an unpredictable thing.

It's why I stand here, head full
of ineffable ideas, ballpoint arms
with no ink left for our song.

You mesmeric conjurer of dust storms
and midnight dances. I know I am too still
for your hobo heart. I know I am too much
metal and not enough earth. I tried to love you
organically. I swear I tried to make a home
of all these scraps.

PICNIC

He always thought she called him Bear
out of love, cherished the way she'd fold herself
around him, rest against his loud loud chest.

Everyone wants a teddy bear
when it's raining outside and the lights
go out. At the dentist. That first month
in a cold bed twenty miles west of home.

But when the weather is nice and the blanket
is smoothed out under a tree, wicker basket heavy
with sweet bread and Dubliner cheese, a local red:
no one wants the Bear, then.

And what is left to do with such a meal
but learn to eat alone?

ORIGIN STORY

I can trace my sadness
back to the Holocaust Museum
and that dying hall of shoes,
the stories of babies thrown
against brick walls and into the air
like clay at the firing range. The pieces
of my sanity have been blown apart
since the second grade, each
shatter moving farther and farther
from the core of what was once
a happy child.

Depression is a sort of ghost,
a thing that lives and does not live.
Each time a stranger names grief
over the crack of a campfire
or in the echo of an empty room
everything good inside me jumps
out of my skin and runs until I am
only this. My heart a scatter plot
of empty shoes and broken bodies.

THE DAY
SHE BURNED

THE TREE IS FROM A FIT OF SEEDS

the tire is from a burned out El Camino
grandpa used to haul firewood up the hill

the dress is from a linen tablecloth
great grandma used for church potlucks

the stain is from the cotton fields
that kept three generations fed

the tear is from the pink depression glass
mom keeps in the corner curio cabinet

the swan dive is from the day she burned
all the blackberries to the ground

the swan dive is from the day
she burned

THE ARTIST
SETS DOWN
HER PEN

The black smack of ink
on her dress bent her double,

a half moon hurling itself
through the air.

Even the birds could not tell
if she had learned to fly

or simply stopped falling
from every hotel room

like a penny at the well
wishing only to be still.

WHEN ONE TWIN CONTEMPLATES SUICIDE

Constance lived one foot
off the roof. Ruth lived
one foot on. Both dressed
sleek as midnight and
never left home without

the pearls mother pulled
apart and divvied
so the two would stop
hanging each other
in the powder room.

Constance leapt from ledge
after ledge without
a solitary
care. Poor Ruth reached for
the awning every time.

Once, a year now past
Constance swallowed pills,
the second attempt
to stomach her grief.
Still, she could not die.

There's a part of her
that just won't let go
and so Constance holds
her sullen siren
song deep in her chest.

Ruth never quiets
the quell between them
but her grip grows strong
enough to hold them
both when Constance falls.

THE NOTE
TAPED TO
THE LOCKER

Row boats and oars
have no place
in the sea, but then
I never meant
to make it back.

Sharks feel the pulse
of empty vessels and the thrash
of frenzied limbs in swells,
the chest full of stones,
the horizon and the shoreline
swallowed by Poseidon.

Whole summers drift by
at the end of the docks
with bottles and lungs
broken into the drink.

I am a buoy dressed in paisley
and red shoes when they come
looking for the girl left to the blue.

JOURNEY TO THE WHALES

past the gap in the window panes/past the empty bird feeder/past the broken tree branch/past the helicopter sputtering overhead/past the burnt out forests and towns/ past the red river/past concrete highways and black skies/past the nuclear power plant/past oil slicks and the spring breakers/past the mouth of the gulf/past the waves breaking in the wind/past the sea gulls and the fishing boats/past the nets/past the stretched out arm of the sun/past all that is not holy/and into the belly of the song

ASHES TO ASHES

Grief is too often a tight rope of stoicism
and unbecoming.

For the guests she wore a black gown,
thumbed the chain around her neck like a rosary.

Mouthed a few words to a song she once knew
by heart. Perched at the front of a room,
urn knocking against her ribs like a lover.

An entire life
small and fleeting
as a fistful of dust.

She closed her eyes until the room
was midnight and fog and harvest moon.

The crag she stood upon was an empty bed
in the middle of winter. Her dress billowed
and stirred, ravens rising one after another
into the battered sky.

She is still and elegant in her anguish,
each heavy breath a blackbird
born from the seams of her resolve.

SAY ITS NAME AND IT WILL COME

The village calls it the darkest May
Day in history, speaks of a haunting
just past the tree line on the far side
of town, grass bending and flattening
underneath a shrill wind song.

He roosts at the top of the maypole,
marking the children who spin round
in circles, ribbons weaving together
an ancestry of ghosts, a lineage
born of bright colors and dancing.

His walking stick becomes a scythe,
wax coat and oil cloth a black robe.
The words plague doctor condense
and rewrite themselves reaper.

He is not a human being
in their stories. No one had ever
even seen the face of the man.

They remember only hollows dark
as pitch where his eyes should be,
beak sharp and curved as a sickle,
the scent of garlic and camphor
wherever he walked.

If he ever had a name, it is gone.
Was he even a man? Who could say?
Now they call it Pesta. Memitim.
Azrael. Santa Muerte. Death.

The story crosses oceans and fords
rivers, learns how to tell itself
in every language. At the center,
a birch tree and children and song.

A village on its knees.

JESUS BLESSING THE TRIBBLES

They came together like a lesson
in exponents, an immaculate reunion
of the fatherless. Bastard children born
onto the hillside new and pure and swelling.

Generations bounded out like fuzzy nesting dolls,
each one eager to sit on His lap. The soft patter
of a few soon thundered toward cacophony.

They wanted to know, is there room enough
for everyone? And He said yes. Are there
enough beds? Enough pillows and blankets?
Will there be enough food? Enough chairs
at the table?

Yes, and yes, and yes, He said,
and the mountain held its breath.

LEGENDARY

I WAS BORN A WET AND UGLY THING

My mother cried at the red bulb
screaming itself blue on her chest.

I tell every lover this story
eventually. Give them an image
to hold when I name my war:

Bipolar.

My bad days are a black
black sea forever too dark
save the hard bright of life
that is not mine.

On my bad days,
I am the sour fountain,
the doomsday prediction at the wedding.

I have eight arms and three hearts;
nothing I hold close wants to stay.

My hearts knock against my soft belly
like old friends.

On the other side of the planet,
I am a busy garden. My arms
are heavy with passion flowers.

BLUEPRINT

We make tradition of dead and dying things.
Deer stands and camouflage. Bass boats
and Baptist churches.

Victrolas whine old Opry songs.
Candelabras thick with tarnish and soot
from last Christmas sit cold and hungry
for the tapered wax of another holiday.

The living rooms in my family all look
the same. Ten point bucks in leisure suits,
puffing their pipes in easy chairs.

At the center, my grandfather.
Twelve years removed from a heart attack
that would kill an ordinary man. New hip,
five teeth, lungs full of lime dust. Clock tower
to this city, every building a history of his resolve.

Grandmother tells the story of the move East
again. Car so small she and three sisters
had to ride in the boot.

Her body is heavy with wolves. She knows
this will be her last winter. Traces our name
past the Trail of Tears, past Revolutionary War,
past the home a man with too many greats
to remember sold to Shakespeare.

This city is a story. Grandfather is not done
building. Grandmother is still writing.

METAMORPHOSIS

I am in my late twenties when I see
a live buck for the first time.

It is running across the state highway
just before dawn, its shoulders
full of shadows and strength.

I have only ever known the end
of its grace, the taxidermy and sport
and trophy hanging above every
dinner table in the family.

The first spring after my daughters
are born holds too many drives
in the dark morning.

Every sharp turn is a tree branch or vine
collecting the colors of rebirth.

I wave to the pockets of deer along
the road, marvel the way daybreak
shifts antlers into bloom.

HIS GRANDKIDS HAD NEVER SEEN HIM LIKE THIS. HE HAD NEVER WORN A BEARD.

Walt had asphalt for skin
despite the wide-brimmed hat
most assumed he had
never taken off.

His eyes narrowed from
the sweat and the sun
until he forgot what it was
to see a thing without focus
and furrowed brow.

The morning after he sold his house
on the hill, the one he built with
his first and last love, he woke
to buttercups and irises on his chin.

When he walked outside, bees buzzed
around him, a thrumming cloud.
Hummingbirds stopped for a drink.

He held out his hand
and expected to see a branch
but it was only a nest
of arthritic knuckles.

A black-bordered lemon moth
landed and looked him
right in the eye. He remembered
a yellow dress and a picnic
years ago.

Spoke to the moth like it was
an old friend. Said goodbye
to the hill, the strawberries,
the green beans and the house.

Crossed the cattle-guard. Opened
and shut the gate one last time.
Walked out into the field with a basket
some bread, a pitcher of blackberry juice.

Sat on the quilt for a long time
before removing his hat
running a hand through his hair
and giving himself to the afternoon.

FLIGHTLESS I

There are three volunteers.

We spend hours on the math.
Calculate the density of helium
and the exact number of red balloons
each pilot will need.

They stand still as tiny rockets
on the launch pad. Each one dressed
to the nines. Black tie.

We wind the string around the volunteers
with awkward precision, all the more difficult
since evolution denied us the dexterity
of fingers and thumbs.

They rise. Higher and higher
until the bouquets above them
are distant hearts.

Our romance with the earth ends.
We line up like dominoes. Waiting.

There was a word once.
It rolls past our children like an antique.
They will never quite understand its power.
Its refusal. The definition of ceilings.

They will only ever know
we will not be this. We will not stand
with our necks bent towards a heaven
that was not meant for us.

We will take every bit of this life.
We will fly.

FLIGHTLESS II

Three penguins fixed themselves to red balloons
and lifted into the atmosphere like teddy bears
outgrown and gifted to cumulus clouds.

Ordinary balloons burst under pressure.
A hard lesson for kings laying claim to Canaan.

They wouldn't make the same mistake twice. This time
they wove reeds and gathered sand, coaxed Prometheus
from the dusty pages of mythology and into an envelope
blue and wide as their conquest. Called upon the dodo
to pull itself from Mauritian swamps.

The ostrich was an easy sell. Heavy chests pine
for weightlessness. He didn't ask where or why
or how. Didn't need to understand the science
of refusal.

Together they climbed in and set fire to the air.
Rewrote themselves legendary.

EVOLUTION

It begins simple, as it always does. A teacher
or parent uses the words real world and swears
it's not cynicism, it's realism. Eyes narrow,
arms flex and tense. The thing that can't be done
is done. It's the sort of obstinate evolution
only a jaded mentor could spark.

The giant octopus is deep sea. It knows black
water and fish like neon signs, but it does not
know sunlight or trees or white-tailed deer
or great blue herons. It does not know roots.

It does not know these things
until it does.

Science is a magician who reveals her tricks.

The trick: tell a massive invertebrate it will never know
a nervous system hard as bone or the ecosystem
of a southern marsh. Sit back and watch tentacles
split and thicken, sprout seedlings, build a patch
of ground solid enough for hooves and talons.
See it become everything we said it could not be.

AMELIA

Somewhere a plane swims through a sky as blue
as the water beneath it. Eyes focus and unfocus
against whitecaps two thousand feet below
and the smallest glimmers set their course.

Hope is a school of fish on a sunny day.

They will not find me, there.
They will not find me for centuries.

The stories will swell until whole islands
are swallowed up and the undoing
of the word terrestrial is a legend.

My navigator is an anonymous letter
in a bottle at sea. No one remembers
his name. Our heading. The last transmission.

White noise. I whistle. White noise.

We are a broken marriage
two voices without language.

And so it is that I am a woman without
a country, a grave without a body.
A pilot without wings enough
to come home.

NARWHAL

Analise had been casting nets for years,
but she knew what Peter Parker never would:
Most people don't need a hero. Most people
are strong enough to save themselves.

When you can hold onto anything,
vengeance is a rose bush that won't flower.
It spreads out along the fence line sharp
and dying.

When you can hold onto anything,
it takes practice to let go of the ones
who only ever want to see you
breaking.

Analise stood behind a screen door
with a shotgun and told her first husband
she'd put a bullet in his heart
if she ever saw him again.

It took an ocean
a dinghy
a constellation of starfish
a sea-faring unicorn

but she made peace with herself;
somewhere in New York City

Peter Parker studies the diving bell,
how it engineers an atmosphere
at the bottom of the bay.

RHINOCEROS

And so it carries her across the dry dirt
of a desert three times the size of Earth.

The ghost heart smooths itself out
before her. Loses mass until it is round
as an egg. Her arm is a constellation
of cramped tendons and bone.

He looks through the telescope at his bedside
and watches the pinprick hero gallop
across her barren moon.

The days tick by loud and nagging. Soon
she cannot remember the year. The name
of the animal beneath her. The crook of his neck.

She visits only once every seven years.
Trades the heavy and wheezing hollow
of his chest for the small planet in her hand.

Her own heart bends and unbends its edges,
learns the gravity of empty spaces.

MERONYMY

Fluorescent bulbs blink like fireflies or stars. Hard to say. The whole damn camp is a funhouse. No one comes here to gain perspective. We're in the business of losing. Abigail holds an elephant in her palm like a moon. The menagerie spins round riderless. Everything has a sun of sorts. Even the ferris wheel is stuck in orbit, she thinks. The jack rabbit passes by again like an alien satellite and she remembers the shape of an animal she used to chase from the vegetable patch. The long ears stiffening when her toes dug into the topsoil. It was smaller, then. Her lungs burn. She takes a deep breath and knows it is the last bit of air she will taste. Funny, now, to think of it. She'd never really tasted air. It slips over her tongue like an undergarment over skin. The elephant in her hand lifts its trunk. Shifts its weight. She peers into its eyes and sees that each one is a crocus in early Spring. The sky is a hard silence. She thinks of home. Wonders how she ever came to this place, why it feels like returning.

ABOUT THE ILLUSTRATOR

Influenced by personal trauma and struggles with depression and anxiety disorders, Desarae creates work that revolves around themes of finding humor in pain, beauty in the grotesque, and light in the darkness. As comfortable referencing geek culture as she is bearing the depths of her soul, Desarae's work ranges in theme but is always, as she says, "an attempt to connect the hidden places in myself to the hidden places in the viewer, to somehow create a bridge of communication over the immense expanse of our differing perceptions, beliefs, and experiences." Desarae's technique revolves around using line to create value and texture. Working primarily with pen and ink, Desarae balances exact, meticulous line-work with natural, flowing compositions. Over time, her work has developed to include watercolor, tea-staining, and print-making. It is within this juxtaposition of controlled pen and unpredictable watercolor that Desarae finds her voice. Desarae's work begs you to understand her innermost being and through that gives you the courage to examine your own.

ABOUT THE AUTHOR

Ronnie K. Stephens teaches English and English as a Second Language in Texas. He has identical twins and a brand new baby that take up all the space in his chest. Currently, he is pursuing an MFA in Creative Writing from Wilkes University and writing a novel about the indomitable spirit of young women with guidance from Kaylie Jones. Once complete, he will turn his attention to a memoir chronicling his experiences with bipolar disorder and how they've shaped him as a father. He also manages Dad Arms, a blog on parenting. His first collection, Universe in the Key of Matryoshka, was published by Timber Mouse Publishing in 2014.

ACKNOWLEDGMENTS

The author would like to thank: Mallerie, for reminding him daily that he is enough; Zachary Campbell, without whom Desarae and I would have never met; Dane Kutler, for being the wisest, most intuitive friend and editor he knows; the editors of Elsewhere Literary Magazine, Split Lip Magazine, Kentucky Review, SPRY, Freezeray Poetry, and The Good Men Project, who gave space to some of the poems in this book long before the project came to fruition; his children, for being the most frustrating and constant source of joy; Desarae, for a decade of friendship, healing, and endless inspiration.

CPSIA information can be obtained
at www.ICGtesting.com
Printed in the USA
BVHW020757020119
536808BV00006B/4/P